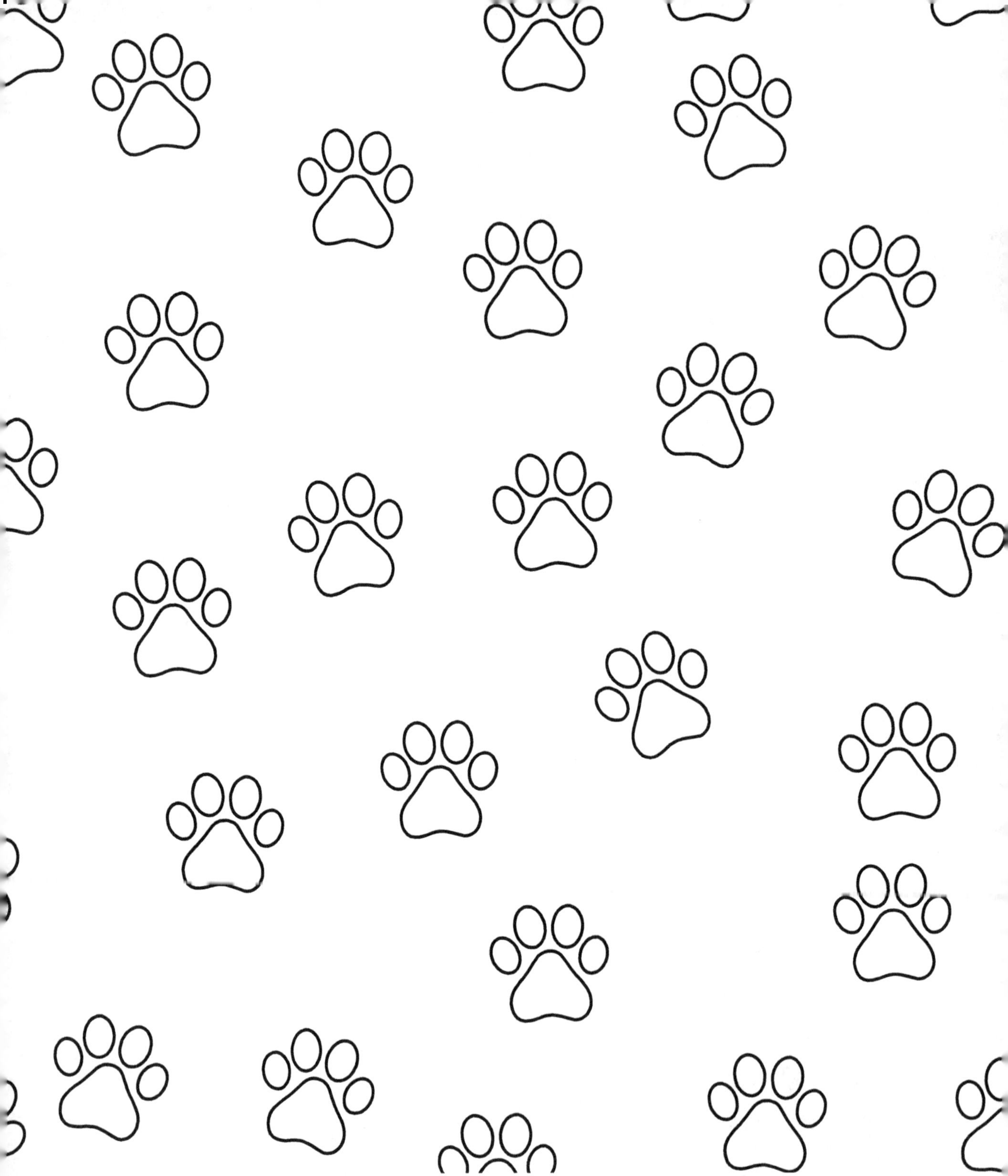

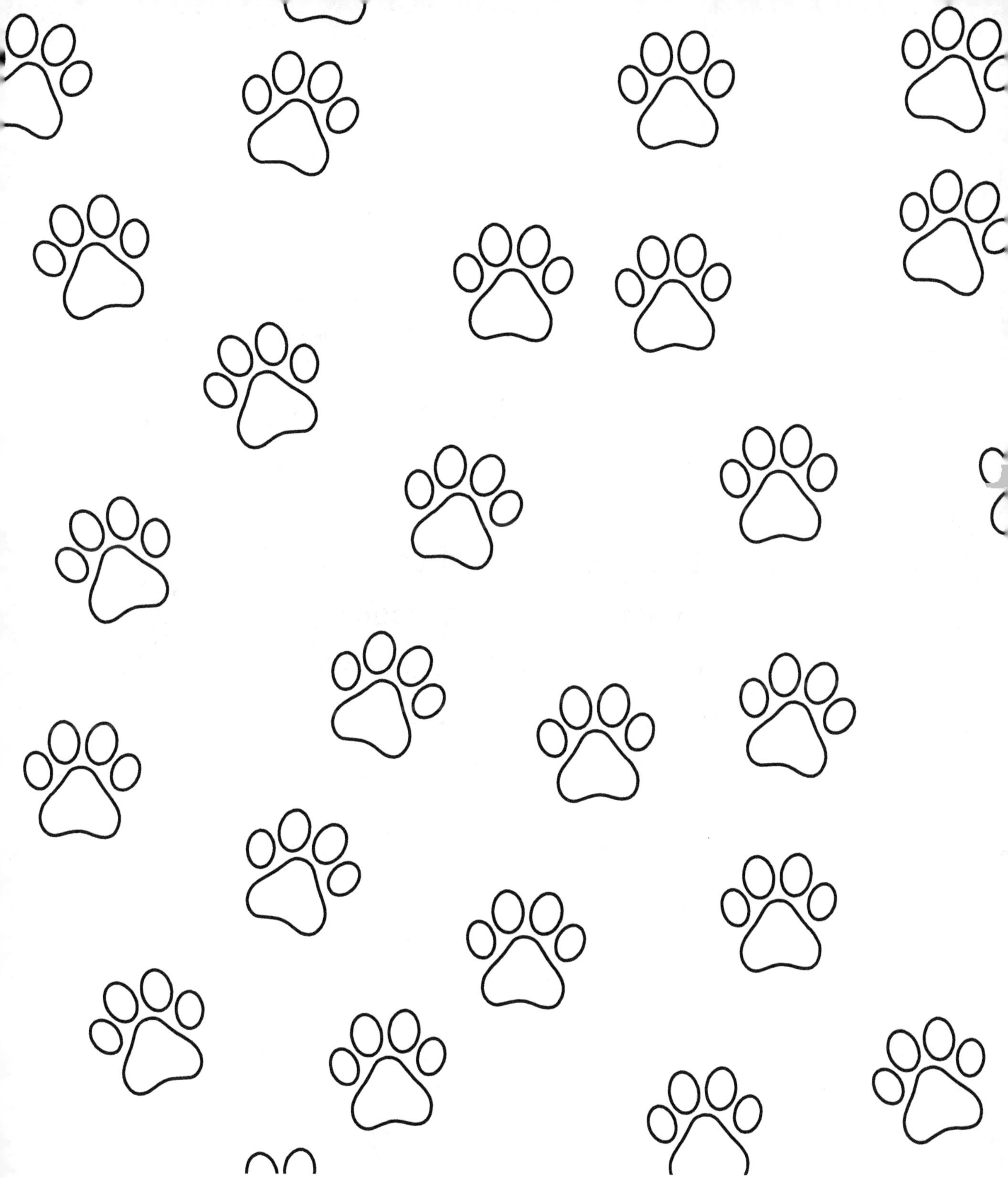

Dedicated to my Nana & Pop-Pop,
who never stopped believing in me.

And in loving memory of Jeter Scott -
a sweet, fluffy, big-headed,
floppy-eared, yellow labrador
who was everyone's friend,
and his mom's first love.

This book is given with love:

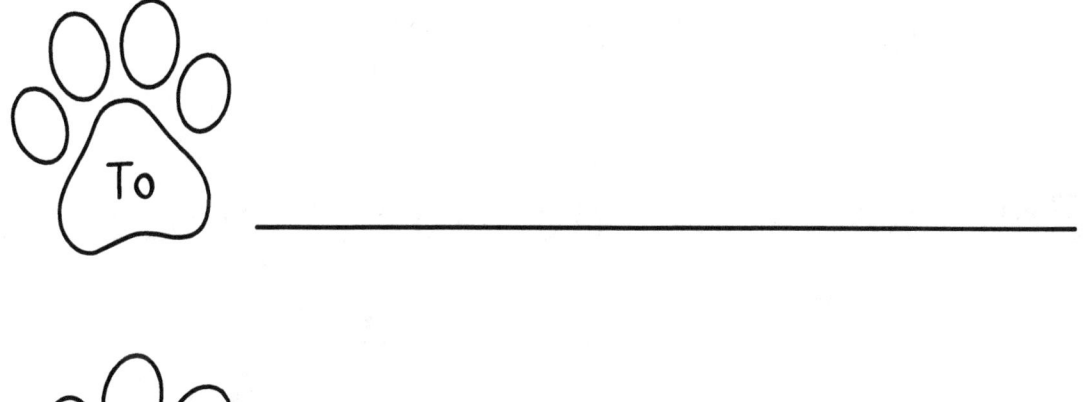

To _____

From _____

May we not just learn
life's most important lessons,
but live them every day.

Pay more attention to our people.
Take time to rest.
Find joy in the little things.

May you sit longer with those
who make you happy.

Stay awhile in the places
that bring you joy.

And love greater than yesterday,
for the days go fast.

Copyright © 2021 by Puppy Dogs & Ice Cream, Inc.
All rights reserved. Published in the United States
by Puppy Dogs & Ice Cream, Inc.
ISBN: 978-1-957922-07-2
Edition: January 2021

For all inquiries, please contact us at:
info@puppysmiles.org

To see more of our books, visit us at:
www.PuppyDogsAndIceCream.com

SIT. STAY.
LOVE.

Life Lessons from a Doggie

Written by: Chalaine Kilduff   Illustrated by: Sally Brodermann

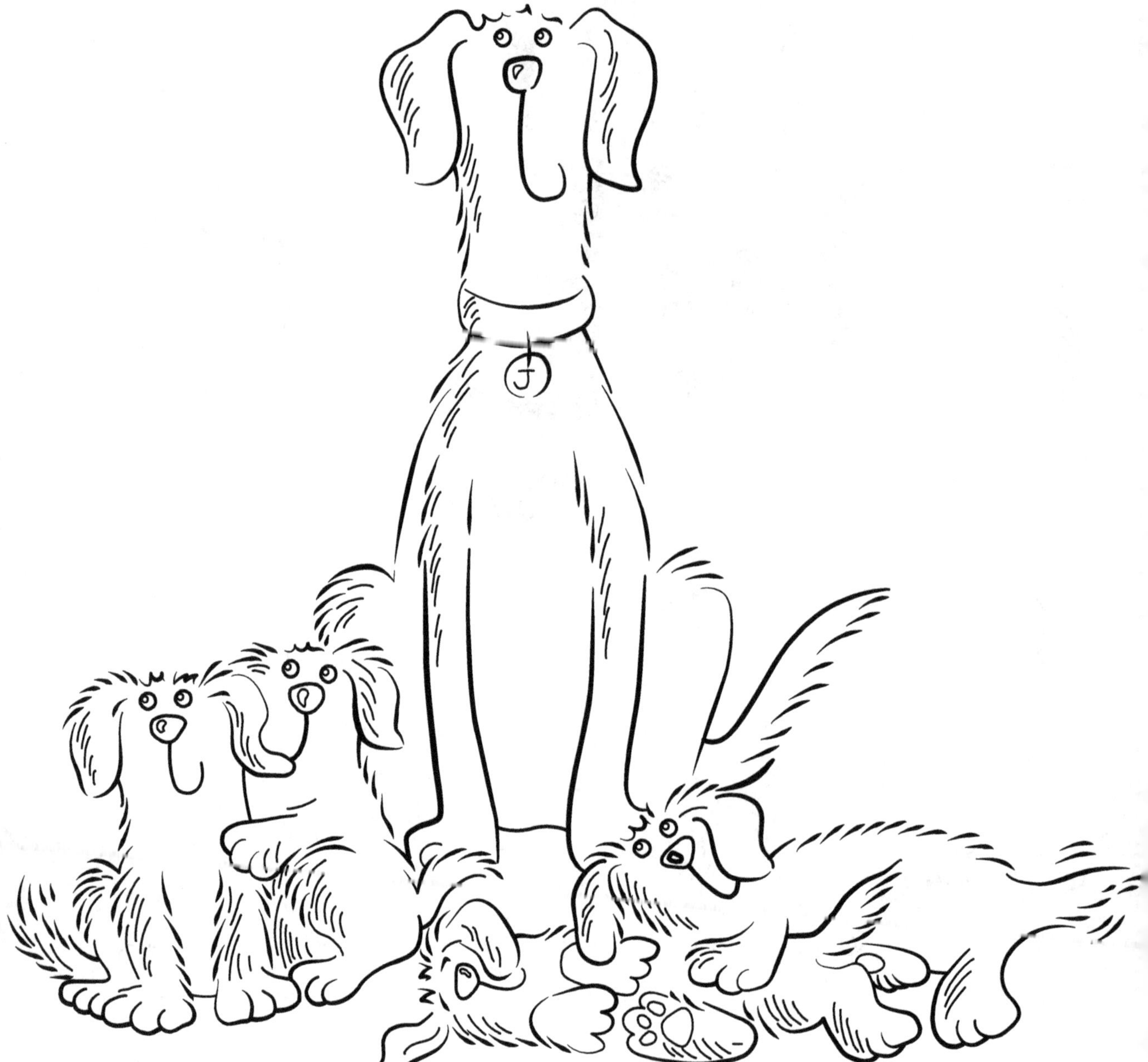
J

There's so much to learn
as you grow up...
Sometimes, the best lessons
can come from a pup.

As you get big
and strong
and wise...

Remember that courage doesn't come from your size.

Do the right thing,
even when it's hard...

Don't go with strangers,
and stay close to your yard.

Obey authority
and give respect
where it's due...

Always remember that God's watching you.

Do your chores,
and pick up your mess...

Give what you can
to those who have less.

Share your toys
and take time to play...

Be sure to get your rest after a long day.

Whenever you can,
offer lots of snugs...

Give your best humans
all of the hugs.

Love with all you can
and with all your might...

Be kind to others,
and do not fight.

Be a great listener
and always do good...

Never sit down
when you should have stood.

BAD WAY GOOD WAY

Guide your feet
where they should go...

Follow your heart,
and lead it so.

Say your prayers every night...

When it's dark, be the light.

Be a blessing
and help others out...

That's what life is all about!

Hebraic Characters Considered As Signs

Fabre D'Olivet

Kessinger Publishing's Rare Reprints

Thousands of Scarce and Hard-to-Find Books on These and other Subjects!

- Americana
- Ancient Mysteries
- Animals
- Anthropology
- Architecture
- Arts
- Astrology
- Bibliographies
- Biographies & Memoirs
- Body, Mind & Spirit
- Business & Investing
- Children & Young Adult
- Collectibles
- Comparative Religions
- Crafts & Hobbies
- Earth Sciences
- Education
- Ephemera
- Fiction
- Folklore
- Geography
- Health & Diet
- History
- Hobbies & Leisure
- Humor
- Illustrated Books
- Language & Culture
- Law
- Life Sciences
- Literature
- Medicine & Pharmacy
- Metaphysical
- Music
- Mystery & Crime
- Mythology
- Natural History
- Outdoor & Nature
- Philosophy
- Poetry
- Political Science
- Science
- Psychiatry & Psychology
- Reference
- Religion & Spiritualism
- Rhetoric
- Sacred Books
- Science Fiction
- Science & Technology
- Self-Help
- Social Sciences
- Symbolism
- Theatre & Drama
- Theology
- Travel & Explorations
- War & Military
- Women
- Yoga
- *Plus Much More!*

**We kindly invite you to view our catalog list at:
http://www.kessinger.net**

THIS ARTICLE WAS EXTRACTED FROM THE BOOK:

Hebraic Tongue Restored Part 1

BY THIS AUTHOR:

Fabre D'Olivet

ISBN 0766126064

READ MORE ABOUT THE BOOK AT OUR WEB SITE:

http://www.kessinger.net

OR ORDER THE COMPLETE
BOOK FROM YOUR FAVORITE STORE

ISBN 0766126064

CHAPTER III.

CHARACTERS CONSIDERED AS SIGNS.

§ I.

TRACED CHARACTERS, ONE OF THE ELEMENTS OF LANGUAGE:

HIEROGLYPHIC PRINCIPLE OF THEIR PRIMITIVE FORM.

We are about to examine the alphabetical form and value of the Hebrew characters; let us fix our attention now upon the meaning which is therein contained. This is a matter somewhat novel and I believe it has not been properly investigated.

According to Court de Gébelin, the origin of speech is divine. God alone can give to man the organs which are necessary for speaking; He alone can inspire in him the desire to profit by his organs; He alone can establish between speech and that multitude of marvelous objects which it must depict, that admirable *rapport* which animates speech, which makes it intelligible to all, which makes it a picture with an energy and truthfulness that cannot be mistaken. This estimable writer says, "How could one fail to recognize here the finger of the All Powerful? how could one imagine that words had no energy by themselves? that they had no value which was not conventional and which might not always be different; that the name of lamb might be that of wolf, and the name of vice that of virtue, etc."[1]

[1] *Monde primi. Orig. du lang.* p. 66.

Indeed a person must be the slave of system, and singularly ignorant of the first elements of language to assert with Hobbes and his followers, that there is nothing which may not be arbitrary in the institution of speech;[2] that "we cannot from experience conclude that anything is to be called just or unjust, true or false, or any proposition universal whatsoever, except it be from remembrance of the use of names imposed arbitrarily by men."[3]

Again if Hobbes, or those who have followed him, having delved deeply in the elements of speech, had demonstrated the nothingness or absolute indifference of it by a rational analysis of tongues or even simply by the analysis of the tongue that they spoke; but these men, compilers of certain Latin words, believed themselves so wise that the mere declaration of their paradox was its demonstration. They did not suspect that one could raise his grammatical thoughts above a supine or a gerund.

May I be pardoned for this digression which, distant as it appears from the Hebraic grammar, brings us, however, back to it; for it is in this grammar that we shall find the consoling proof, stated above by Gébelin and the response to the destructive paradoxes of Hobbes and all his acolytes. It is even one of the motives which has caused me to publish this grammar, and which, being connected with that of giving to my translation of the Cosmogony of Moses an incontrovertible basis, engages me in a work to which I had not at first destined myself.

I shall show that the words which compose the tongues in general, and those of the Hebraic tongue in particular, far from being thrown at hazard, and formed by the explosion of an arbitrary caprice, as has been asserted, are, on the contrary, produced by a profound reason. I shall prove that there is not a single one that may not, by means of a well made grammatical analysis

[2] Hobb. *de la nat. hum.* ch. 4. 10.
[3] *Ibid*: ch. 5. § 10. Leviath. ch. 4.

be brought back to the fixed elements of a nature, immutable as to substance, although variable to infinity as to forms.

These elements, such as we are able to examine here, constitute that part of speech to which I have given the name of *sign*. They comprise, as I have said, the voice, the gesture, and the traced characters. It is to the traced characters that we shall apply ourselves; since the voice is extinct, and the gesture disappeared. They alone will furnish us a subject amply vast for reflections.

According to the able writer whom I have already quoted, their form is by no means arbitrary. Court de Gébelin proves by numerous examples that the first inventors of the literal alphabet, unique source of all the literal alphabets in actual use upon the earth, and whose characters were at first only sixteen in number, drew from nature itself the form of these characters, relative to the meaning which they wished to attach to them. Here are his ideas upon this subject, to which I shall bring only some slight changes and certain developments necessitated by the extent of the Hebraic alphabet and the comparison that I am obliged to make of several analogous letters; in order to reduce the number to the sixteen primordial characters, and make them harmonize with their hieroglyphic principle.

א A.—Man himself as collective unity, principle: master and ruler of the earth.

בפ B. P. PH.—The mouth of man as organ of speech; his interior, his habitation, every central object.

גכ G. C. CH.—The throat: the hand of man half closed and in action of taking: every canal, every enclosure, every hollow object.

דת D. DH. TH.—The breast: every abundant, nutritive object: all division, all reciprocity.

ה H. EH. AH.—The breath: all that which animates: air, life, being.

ע O. U.—The eye: all that which is related to the light, to brilliancy, to limpidness, to water.

עו OU. W. WH.—The ear: all that which is related to sound, to noise, to wind: void, nothingness.

שׂםן Z. S. SH.—A staff, an arrow, a bow; the arms, the instruments of man: every object leading to an end.

ח H. HE. CH.—A field, image of natural existence: all that which requires work, labour, effort: all that which excites heat.

טצ T. TZ.—A roof: a place of surety, of refuge: a haven, a shelter; a term, an aim: an end.

י I.—The finger of man, his extended hand: all that which indicates the directing power and which serves to manifest it.

ל L.—The arm: everything which is extended, raised, displayed.

מ M.—The companion of man, woman: all that which is fruitful and creative.

נ N.—The production of woman: a child: any fruit whatsoever: every produced being.

ק Q. K.—A positive arm: all that which serves, defends, or makes an effort for man.

ר R.—The head of man: all that which possesses in itself, a proper and determining movement.

Now it must be observed that these characters received these symbolic figures from their first inventors only because they already contained the idea; that in passing to the state of signs, they present only abstractly to the thought the faculties of these same objects: but, as I have stated, they can fulfill the functions of the *signs*, only after having been veritable *nouns:* for every *sign* manifested exteriorly is at first a *noun*.

§ II.

ORIGIN OF SIGNS AND THEIR DEVELOPMENT:

THOSE OF THE HEBRAIC TONGUE.

Let us try to discover how the *sign*, being manifested exteriorly, produced a *noun*, and how the *noun*, characterized by a figured type produced a *sign*. Let us take for example, the sign מ M, which, expressing by means of its primordial elements, the sound and organs of the voice, becomes the syllable aM or Ma, and is applied to those faculties of woman which eminently distinguish her, that is to say, to those of mother. If certain minds attacked by skepticism ask me why I restrict the idea of mother in this syllable aM or Ma, and how I am sure that it is applied effectively there, I shall reply to them that the sole proof that I can give them, in the material sphere which envelops them is, that in all the tongues of the world from that of the Chinese to that of the Caribs, the syllable aM or Ma is attached to the idea of mother, and aB, Ba, or aP, Pa, to that of father. If they doubt my assertion let them prove that it is false; if they do not doubt it, let them tell me how it is that so many diverse peoples, thrown at such distances apart, unknown to each other, are agreed in the signification of this syllable, if this syllable is not the innate expression of the sign of maternity.

This is a grammatical truth that all the sophisms of Hobbes and his disciples knew not how to overthrow.

Let us settle upon this fundamental point and proceed. What are the relative or abstract ideas which are attached to, or which follow from, the primordial idea represented by the syllable aM or Ma? Is it not the idea of fecundity, of multiplicity, of abundance? Is it not the idea of fecundation, of multiplication, of formation? Does not one see from this source, every idea of excited and passive action, of exterior movement, of plastic force, of characteristic place, of home, of means, etc?

It is useless to pursue this examination: the mass of ideas contained in the primordial idea of mother, is either attached to the figured sign, to the typical character which represents it, or is derived from and follows it.

Each *sign* starts from the same principles and acquires the same development. Speech is like a sturdy tree which, shooting up from a single trunk begins with a few branches; but which soon extends itself, spreads, and becomes divided in an infinity of boughs whose interlaced twigs are blended and mingled together.

And do not wonder at this immense number of ideas following from so small a number of *signs*. It is by means of the eight keys called *Koua,* that the Chinese tongue, at first reduced to two hundred and forty primordial characters, is raised to eighty and even eighty-four thousand derivative characters, as I have already said.

Now the newer a tongue is and closer to nature, the more the *sign* preserves its force. This force dies out insensibly, in proportion as the derivative tongues are formed, blended, identified and mutually enriched with a mass of words which, belonging to several tribes at first isolated and afterward united, lose their synonymy and finally are coloured with all the nuances of the imagination, and adapt themselves to every delicacy of sentiment and expression. The force of the *sign* is the grammatical touchstone by means of which one can judge without error the antiquity of any tongue.

In our modern tongues, for example, the *sign*, because of the idiomatic changes brought about by time, is very difficult to recognize; it yields only to a persistent analysis. It is not thus in Hebrew. This tongue, like a vigorous shoot sprung from the dried trunk of the primitive tongue, has preserved on a small scale all the forms and all the action. The *signs* are nearly all evident, and many even are detached: when this is the case, I shall give them name of *relations* for I understand by *sign* only the constitutive character of a root, or the character which placed at the beginning or at the end of a word, modifies its expression without conserving any in itself.

I now pass, after these explanations, to what the Hebraic *signs* indicate, that is to say, to a new development of the literal characters of the Hebraic tongue considered under the relation of the primitive ideas which they express, and by which they are constituted representative *signs* of these same ideas.

א A.—This first character of the alphabet, in nearly all known idioms, is the sign of power and of stability. The ideas that it expresses are those of unity and of the principle by which it is determined.

ב B. P.—Virile and paternal sign: image of active and interior action.

ג G.—This character which offers the image of a canal, is the organic sign; that of the material covering and of all ideas originating from the corporeal organs or from their action.

ד D.—Sign of nature, divisible and divided: it expresses every idea proceeding from the abundance born of division.

ה H. He.—Life and every abstract idea of being.

ו OU. W.—This character offers the image of the most profound, the most inconceivable mystery, the image of the knot which unites, or the point which separates nothingness and being. It is the universal, convertible sign which makes a thing pass from one nature to another; communicating on the one side, with the sign of light and of spiritual sense ו, which is itself more elevated, and connecting on the other side, in its degeneration, with the sign of darkness and of material sense ע which is itself still more abased.

ז Z. C. S.—Demonstrative sign: abstract image of the link which unites things: symbol of luminous refraction.

ח H. HE. CH.—This character, intermediary between ה and כ, the former designating life, absolute existence; the latter, relative life, assimilated existence.—is the sign of elementary existence: it offers the image of a sort of equilibrium, and is attached to ideas of effort, of labour, and of normal and of legislative action.

ט T.—Sign of resistance and of protection. This character serves as link between ד and ת, which are both much more expressive.

י I.—Image of potential manifestation: of spiritual duration, of eternity of time and of all ideas relating thereunto: remarkable character in its vocal nature, but which loses all of its faculties in passing to the state of consonant, wherein it depicts no more than a material duration, a sort of link as ו, or of movement as שׁ.

כ C. CH.—Assimilative sign: it is a reflective and transient life, a sort of mould which receives and makes all forms. It is derived from the character ח which proceeds itself from the sign of absolute life ה. Thus holding, on the one side, to elementary life, it joins to the signification of the character ח, that of the organic sign ג, of which it is, besides, only a kind of reinforcement.

ל L.—Sign of expansive movement: it is applied to all

ORIGIN OF SIGNS OF HEBRAIC TONGUE

ideas of extension, elevation, occupation, possession. As final sign, it is the image of power derived from elevation.

מ **M.**—Maternal and female sign: local and plastic sign: image of exterior and passive action. This character used at the end of words, becomes the collective sign ם. In this state, it develops the being in indefinite space, or it comprises, in the same respect, all beings of an identical nature.

נ **N.**—Image of produced or reflected being: sign of individual and of corporeal existence. As final character it is the augmentative sign ן, and gives to the word which receives it all the individual extension of which the expressed thing is susceptible.

ס **S. X.**—Image of all circumscription: sign of circular movement in that which has connection with its circumferential limit. It is the link ז reinforced and turned back upon itself.

ע **H. WH.**—Sign of material meaning. It is the sign ו considered in its purely physical relations. When the vocal sound ע, degenerates in its turn into consonant, it becomes the sign of all that which is bent, false, perverse and bad.

פ **PH. F.**—Sign of speech and of that which is related to it. This character serves as link between the characters ב and ו, B and V, when the latter has passed into state of consonant; it participates in all their significations, adding its own expression which is the emphasis.

צ **TZ.**—Final and terminative sign being related to all ideas of scission, of term, solution, goal. Placed at the beginning of words, it indicates the movement which carries toward the term of which it is the sign: placed at the end, it marks the same term where it has tended; then it receives this form ץ, It is derived from the character ם and from the character ן, and it marks equally scission for both.

ק Q. K.—Sign eminently compressive, astringent and trenchant; image of the agglomerating or repressive form. It is the character כ wholly materialized and is applied to objects purely physical. For this is the progression of the signs: ה, universal life; ח, elementary existence, the effort of nature; כ, assimilated life holding the natural forms; ק material existence giving the means of forms.

ר R.—Sign of all movement proper, good or bad: original and frequentative sign: image of the renewal of things as to their movement.

ש SH.—Sign of relative duration and of movement therewith connected. This character is derived from the vocal sound י, passed into the state of consonant; it joins to its original expression the respective significations of the characters ז and ם.

ת TH.—Sign of reciprocity: image of that which is mutual and reciprocal. Sign of signs. Joining to the abundance of the character ר, to the force of the resistance and protection of the character ט, the idea of perfection of which it is itself the symbol.

Twenty-two signs: such are the simple bases upon which reposes the Hebraic tongue, upon which are raised the primitive or derivative tongues which are attached to the same origin. From the perfect understanding of these bases, depends the understanding of their genius: their possession is a key which unlocks the roots.

§ III.

USE OF THE SIGNS: EXAMPLE DRAWN FROM THE FRENCH.

I might expatiate at length upon the signification of each of these characters considered as *Signs*, especially if I had added to the general ideas that they express, some of the particular, relative or abstract ideas which are necessarily attached; but I have said enough for the attentive reader and he will find elsewhere in the course of this work quite a considerable number of examples and developments to assure his progress and level all doubts which he might have conceived.

As I have not yet spoken of the *noun*, fundamental part of speech, and as it would be difficult for those of my readers, who have of the Hebraic tongue only the knowledge that I am giving them, to understand me if I proceeded abruptly to the composition or the decomposition of the Hebraic words by means of the sign, I shall put off demonstrating the form and utility of this labour. In order, however, not to leave this chapter imperfect and to satisfy the curiosity as much as possible, without fatiguing too much the attention, I shall illustrate the power of the sign by a French word, taken at hazard, of a common acceptation and of obvious composition.

Let it be the word *emplacement*.* Only a very super-

* At the very moment of writing this, I was at the *Bureau des Opérations militaires du Ministère de la guerre*, where I was then employed. Just as I was seeking for the French word announced in the above paragraph, the chief of the division interrupted me, in order to give me some work to do relative to an *emplacement* of troops. My administrative labour terminated, I again took up my grammatical work, retaining the same word which had engaged my attention.

ficial knowledge of etymology is necessary to see that the simple word here is *place*. Our first task is to connect it with the tongue from which it is directly derived; by this means we shall obtain an etymology of the first degree, which will set to rights the changes which might be effected in the characters of which it is composed. Now, whether we go to the Latin tongue, or whether we go to the Teutonic tongue, we shall find in the one *platea*, and in the other *platz*. We shall stop there without seeking the etymology of the second degree, which would consist in interrogating the primitive Celt, common origin of the Latin and the Teutonic; because the two words that we have obtained suffice to enlighten us.

It is evident that the constitutive root of the French word *place*, is *aT* or *aTz*. Now, the sign in *at*, indicates to us an idea of resistance or of protection, and in *atz* an idea of term, of limit, of end. It is, therefore, a thing resisting and limited, or a thing protective and final. But what is the sign which governs this root and which makes it a noun, by proceeding from right to left following the Oriental manner? It is the sign L, that of all extension, of all possession. *Lat* is therefore, a thing extended as *lat*, or extended and possessed as *latitude*. This is unimpeachable.

Next, what is the second sign which stamps a new meaning on these words? It is the sign P, that of active and central action; inner and determinative character; which, from the word *lat*, an extended thing, makes a thing of a fixed and determined extent, a *plat*, or a *place* by changing the *t* into *c*, as the etymology of the first degree has proved to us the reality of this change.

Now that we understand clearly in the word *em-placement*, the simple word *place* of which it is composed, let us search for the elements of its composition. Let us examine first the termination *ment*, a kind of adverbial relation, which added to a noun, determines, in French, an action implied. The etymology of the first degree gives us *mens*, in Latin, and *mind* in Teutonic. These two words mutually explain each other, therefore it is unnecessary for us to turn to the second degree of etymology. Whether we take *mens* or *mind*, it remains for us to explore the root *eN* or *iN*, after dropping the initial character M, and the final S or D, that we shall take up further on. To the root *en*, expressing something even in the tongue of the Latins, we shall now direct our attention.

Here we see the sign of absolute life E, and that of reflective or produced existence N, joined together to designate every particular being. This is precisely what the Latin root EN, signfies, *lo, behold;* that is to say, *see; examine* this individual existence. It is the exact translation of the Hebrew הן *hen!* If you add to this root the luminous sign as in the Greek αἰών (*æon*), you will have the individual being nearest to the absolute being; if, on the contrary, you take away the sign of life and substitute that of duration as in the Latin *in,* you will have the most restricted, the most centralized, the most interior being.

But let the root EN be terminated by the conscriptive and circumferential sign S, and we shall obtain *ens*, corporeal mind, the intelligence peculiar to man. Then let us make this word rule by the exterior and plastic sign M, and we shall have the word *mens*, intelligence manifesting itself outwardly and producing. This is the origin of the termination sought for: it expresses the exterior form according to which every action is modified.

As to the initial syllable *em,* which is found at the head of the word *em-place-ment,* it represents the root EN, and has received the character M, only because of the consonant P, which never allows N in front of it, and this, as though the being generated could never be presented prior to the generating being. This syllable comes therefore from the same source, and whether it be derived from the corresponding Latin words *en* or *in*, it always characterizes restricted existence in a determined or inner point.

According to these ideas, if I had to explain the French word *em-place-ment,* I would say that it signifies the proper mode according to which a fixed and determined extent, as *place,* is conceived or is presented exteriorly.

Moreover, this use of the sign which I have just illustrated by a word of the French tongue, is much easier and more sure in the Hebrew, which, possessing in itself nearly all the constitutive elements, only obliges the etymologist on very rare occasions to leave his lexicon; whereas, one cannot analyze a French word without going back to Latin or Teutonic, from which it is derived, and without making frequent incursions into Celtic, its primitive source, and into Greek and Phœnician, from which it has received at different times a great number of expressions.